Elton Jo

David Farr was born in Guil..... 1969. He has written
three plays: *Neville Southall's Washbag* was nominated for
the Verity Bargate Award of 1992; *Max Klapper – A Life
in Pictures* was performed at the Electric Cinema, London,
in 1996; and *Elton John's Glasses* won Best Regional Play
in the Writer's Guild Awards of 1997. He was Artistic
Director of London's Gate Theatre from 1995 to 1998.

DAVID FARR

Elton John's Glasses

faber and faber
LONDON · BOSTON

First published in 1998
by Faber and Faber Limited
3 Queen Square London WC1N 3AU

Typeset by Faber and Faber Ltd
Printed in England by Mackays of Chatham plc, Chatham, Kent

A CIP record for this book
is available from the British Library

ISBN 0-571-19577-6

2 4 6 8 10 9 7 5 3 1

Author's Note

This play began life in a different form and with a different title, *Neville Southall's Washbag*, and was first performed at the Finborough Theatre, London, in 1992, directed by myself. The play was then radically reworked and presented in its current form, under its present title, at the Watford Palace Theatre in June 1997, directed by Terry Johnson.

I would like to thank Terry Johnson, Giles Croft and all the actors involved in the play's life thus far, in particular Will Keen and Will Barton who have faithfully appeared in every incarnation.

Characters

Bill, 31 years old
Dan, 24 years old, his brother
Shaun, 32 years old, in Dan's band
Tim, 21 years old, in Dan's band
Amy, 16 years old, a local football fan
Julie, 35 years old, a local woman

Location of both acts:
Bill's room, Watford.
An almost completely empty room. There is one window
and a front door. Another door leads to a bathroom and
there is a further door leading to the cellar.
In the room there is only one armchair, a TV and video,
and an old mattress on the floor. Perhaps an old oven on
a table. Nothing much else. The walls are in a bad state,
as is the carpet.

Elton John's Glasses was first performed at the Palace Theatre Watford, on 30 May 1997. The cast was as follows:

Bill Tom Mannion
Dan Will Keen
Shaun Will Barton
Tim David Nellist
Amy Kelly Reilly
Julie Gabrielle Glaister

Director Terry Johnson
Designer Tim Shortall
Lighting Designer Judith Greenwood

A new production opened at the Palace Theatre Watford on 16 April 1998 and was subsequently presented on tour and in the West End by Michael Codron and Lee Dean. The cast was as follows:

Bill Brian Conley
Dan Will Keen
Shaun Will Barton
Tim David Nellist
Amy Dawn Bradfield
Julie Gabrielle Glaister

Director Terry Johnson
Designer Tim Shortall
Lighting Designer Simon Opie

Act One

SCENE ONE

Bill sits in his chair watching a videotape on the television. The commentary is from the 1984 F. A. Cup Final between Everton and Watford. It is the moment when the Watford goalkeeper Steve Sherwood drops the ball from a high cross and Andy Gray scores Everton's winning goal. After the goal has gone in, the videotape goes back on a loop to just before the goal and plays it again.

    Bill sits staring at the screen impassively as the goal is repeated and repeated before his eyes. We do not see the goal, only hearing the commentary.

    A doorbell. Bill ignores it.

    A doorbell. Bill ignores it again.

    A knock on the door. A hard knock.

    The letter box opens. We hear, called out:

Dan Bill? Bill?!

    Bill shoots up from his chair. Turns off the video. Composes himself. Goes to open the door. Stops. Goes again. Opens.

Bill Dan.

Dan Bill. Been a long time. I tried to call.

Bill No phone.

Dan Right.

Bill No beard.

Dan No.

Bill Funny. Thought you'd have a beard.

Dan Never had a beard.

Bill Just imagined you would. Something to say 'things have occurred'. Still, no matter. Where've you . . .

Dan Tranmere. Had a gig.

Bill Long way.

Dan Four hours. Did it in four hours.

Bill On your way . . .?

Dan Bristol. Got a gig.

Bill Popping in?

Dan Thought we might stay. For a couple of days. If that's . . .?

Bill Pleasure. Fantastic. Great. (*He bars the door.*) You all right?

Dan Yeah. No, just wondering, if I could, you know . . .?

Pause. Bill lets Dan in.

Bill Fuck. Course you can. Fuck me, leaving you out in the cold like that, you should have forced your way through. Come in, come in.

Dan Cheers.

Bill Takes a good thumping to get me out the way sometimes. Spent too long as a centre-back, that's what it is. Too long in defence. Brought it into my private life, know what I mean? And in this weather. Coldest spring on record. Fact. Put your bag down. Find a spot for it. Make yourself at home.

Dan is staring. Dan sees Bill staring at him.

Dan Nice place.

Bill It's not Buckingham Palace.

Dan No, but it's got . . .

Bill It's not Windsor Castle. That's down the road.

Dan It's got . . .

Bill Character.

Dan Yeah.

Bill You want Windsor Castle, go down the A42. This here is Watford. You're looking good.

Dan You too. You've . . . (*Stops, embarrassed at Bill's paunch.*)

Bill Grown?

Dan No, you'd grown before. You'd grown already, Bill.

Bill You've grown.

Dan Have I?

Bill Little brother! Not so little!

Dan Right. No, you've, you've filled out into yourself. (*Pause.*) You've, you know, really embraced your skin, you're twice the man you were. (*Pause.*) You look great.

Bill Kind of you to say so.

Dan But nothing changes does it? I mean, at the end of six years, I'm still Dan, you're still Bill.

Bill Still Bill, that's me. And you're Dan. Dan Can. Just like you always were. I liked your letters.

Dan Yeah, I'm sorry, I should have written more. Did I write four, five?

Bill Three. Two letters and a postcard. Little gems all of them. I've got them if you want your memory jogging?

3

Dan No, it's fine. (*Pause*.) So, Bill, where is, you know, where is . . .

Bill Hmmn?

Dan You know houses?

Bill Yeah.

Dan Well, normally, not always I grant you, but on the whole, they've got things in them, would you say?

Bill You'll have to help me out here.

Dan You know the sort of thing, possessions, belongings, stuff.

Bill Stuff?

Dan Yeah, you know, cookers, carpets, cushions . . . Doesn't matter.

Bill What are you saying?

Dan Nothing. Forget it.

Bill Are you saying there's nothing in my house?

Dan No! Well, I mean.

Bill Carpets! Cushions!

Dan I like it. I like the look. It's just a new look. That's all.

Bill I've become rather minimalist in my perspective, Dan. I think this room reflects that.

Dan Yeah, it does.

Bill You're not the only one that's been moving on, Dan Can. Still Bill's been moving on in his own inner little way, all right?

Dan Sure. I'm just wondering if we really should stay

here. I mean, we can find somewhere else . . .

Bill What's your problem?

Dan Nothing. It's fine. Really.

Bill Has that bag got one of those newfangled bombs in it that explodes when you put it down?

Dan No. No.

Dan puts his bag down. Bill sits down moodily.

Bill So where's this band then?

Dan The band?

Bill Yeah. Where's the rest of the great success story?

Dan You'll like them, Bill.

Bill How many d'you play to?

Dan On average? Five hundred? Can be a thousand. But remember, that's only the North.

Bill A thousand.

Dan The point is, we're not stopping in the North. At the end of the day the North's just the North. If we were to be honest, it's the poorer relation.

Bill You know that thing they say. 'Never been north of Watford, that one!' Can't say that of you. Can of me, of course. Never have been north of Watford. Thing is, I've never been south of Watford either. Watford through and through. That's me.

Pause.

Dan It's just for the weekend, Bill. The fact is, we can't afford to stay longer. I mean, our schedule won't allow it. It's a pretty packed schedule. So it's just for the weekend.

5

Bill How many are you?

Dan In the band? Four. But we're meeting Josette in Bristol, at the gig. It's a big gig for us, should be a few scouts, you know the score, people from the business, people from Bristol, we've got quite a Bristol sound.

Bill What does Bristol sound like then?

Dan No, the music, Bristol sound. There's a big scene there. Then we'll go to Cardiff maybe. We're sort of nervous about London, don't want to go there too soon. But the point is, Josette's meeting us in Bristol. So it's just me and the lads. Josette's the singer. She's black.

Bill You shagging her?

Dan When it comes to music I like to keep everything on a strictly professional basis, Bill. And Josette respects that.

Bill Does she.

Dan That reminds me, how's, I mean are you still with, what's her name? I've forgotten her name, hairdresser, tall girl, hair all fluffing up like a chocolate mousse . . . Penelope! (*Pause.*) Is it me or is it cold in here?

Bill It's you.

Dan You're not . . . together . . . any more?

Bill No.

Dan My condolences, Bill.

Bill She's not dead.

Dan No, I know.

Bill She went to the Alps. To get a bit of sun.

Dan When?

Bill Three years ago.

6

Dan Oh. Well, I'm sorry you know.

Bill It's no skin off my nose.

Dan Anyone new?

Bill This girl comes round Saturday afternoons for a couple of hours.

Dan What's she like?

Bill She's twenty-two, platinum blonde, with all the enthusiasm that comes with, you know. Physically she's certainly not a disappointment. Pins like roads. Speaking of which, I shall be asking you to vacate the premises for a couple of hours this afternoon.

Dan Absolutely. Twenty-two, eh . . .

Bill Six years. Feels like yesterday.

Dan Hold on . . .

Bill Well, the day before yesterday. Yes?

Dan You're seeing this girl this afternoon?

Bill Yeah.

Dan What about the Hornets?

Bill Hmmn?

Dan What about the football? What about Watford?

Bill What about them?

Dan They're playing today. It's the crunch game!

Bill Is it?

Dan Bill, you never missed a game in ten years! You even saw the reserve games on Thursdays.

Bill Oh. Haven't been for a while.

Dan You what?

Bill Guess it must be . . . four years.

Dan Four years!

Bill Four years three months twenty-six days. Something like that. Yeah, I was watching a game, as per usual, in my usual seat. Not a wildly important game, coming up to Christmas, I think we were languishing in mid-table somewhere under the stupendously inept management of Steve Perryman. Fat chance of promotion, but not much risk of going down. A drab goalless affair. And Luther missed this chance. Near the end.

Dan Luther Blissett.

Bill No, actually it was Martin Luther, Martin Luther King, for Christ's sake. Luther van Dross came on and missed a tap-in. Of course it was Luther fucking Blissett.

Dan Right.

Bill Well, it was a difficult chance and at that time Luther was reaching the autumn of his glittering career, he wasn't quite the athlete of yesteryear. He put it wide. But somehow it just summed it up. I got up, walked out, and I've never been back.

Dan I can't believe it. I was listening to the radio on the way down. It's the big game, last game of the season. It's victory or that's it, curtains. Relegation. I was telling the lads all about it.

Bill I can still hear the roar through the window.

Dan I was saying how pumped up you'd be for the game.

Bill Though it's more often a soft groan these days. Like the whole town's sighing.

Dan And you're not even going!

Bill No, there's only one thing I watch now. It's on that VCR. It's just this moment. I've got it eighty-four times on that video. Made it up myself. I often find myself watching it for hours, hours and hours.

Dan Doesn't that get repetitive?

Bill Of course it gets repetitive. Watching the same thing eight-four times? What I think you mean is does it get monotonous. No, Dan. It actually becomes increasingly meaningful with each viewing.

Dan What's on it?

Pause.

Bill A dream dying.

Dan What dream?

Bill What dream?! Only the greatest fucking fairy tale in football history! Only Graham Taylor and Elton John taking a pissy nowhere fourth division club to the very top. In six years!! Six mad, wonderful, impossible years! Elton John investing a hefty share of the fortune he amassed from his many platinum-selling albums and world tours. Graham Taylor, not only bringing a success hitherto unknown to anyone in the living memory of the club, but also introducing a whole new audience to the game with his revolutionary family enclosures, where children, wives, young and old, the healthy and the lame, the blind, the deaf, the dumb and insane could all join the great Watford crusade: football where everyone had a chance, everyone had a say. Only that. Only that. Only the fucking meek inheriting the fucking earth!

Dan Right.

Bill And then, on one May afternoon, the dream died. Graham Taylor and Elton John led their men to a foot-

9

balling zenith never even considered in the most fertile Watford imagination: the F. A. Cup Final. The Cup Final. THE Wembley Cup Final. The Final. The Mecca of fucking football. And it was there that the dream died.

The bell rings.

Dan That'll be the band.

Bill Watford versus Everton. It was David and Goliath, the little man against the sea of blue. At half-time Watford are one–nil down, a shabby goal scored by a long-haired ape whose name slips my mind. Graham Taylor gathers his men in the Wembley dressing room. He speaks for fourteen minutes, never once raising his voice. To this day no one knows what he said. There are players who were there who can't even remember a single one of those magical words.

The bell rings.

Dan Shall I get it?

Bill Watford are transformed. They tackle with religious fervour, they pass with the faith of the blessed. The aristocrats of Everton, holding on to their slender lead, are getting nervous. Things are turning round.

The bell rings.

Then, out on the right-hand side, the Everton winger Trevor Steven, a balding twat with no brains, picks up the ball and hoofs a high, hopeful centre into the Watford goalmouth. It is a forlorn, empty gesture, meat and drink to the magisterial frame of Steve Sherwood.

Dan Bill, do you think I should . . .?

Dan heads for the door. But . . .

Bill It is at this moment that the May sun comes out from a small cloud, and graces Wembley Stadium with her ebullient warmth. It's every fan's dream and every goal-keeper's nightmare. But Graham Taylor is no fool. Knowing the forecast, he has deliberately ensured that the sun is shining on to the other end, away from Steve Sherwood, in the second half. There should be no problem. There would have been no problem. Had it not been for Elton John's glasses.

Dan Elton John's what?

The bell rings. But Dan turns back to Bill, fascinated.

Bill As Steve Sherwood jumps to collect the cross, Elton John rises to his feet in anxiety. The move is fatal. In mid leap, Steve Sherwood is suddenly blinded by a burning white light flashing across the pitch. It is the glare of the sun reflecting off the huge, gaping expanse of Elton John's glasses. Other players shield their eyes from this terrifying sheet of light. The crowd watch through half-closed eyelids as, his eyes on fire, his head spinning, Steve Sherwood drops the ball, and in the ensuing confusion the Everton striker Andy Gray steals in to score a second and decisive goal. It's over. The Cup is Everton's.

The consequences of that moment are hard to explain. Steve Sherwood is scarred for life. Elton John is devastated; his career and life will enter a period of confusion and sadness resulting in the break-up of his marriage with the lovely Renate. Graham Taylor will never again be the manager he was, stumbling from failure to disaster, and from disaster to Wolves. And Watford FC will never again be the club of dreams, the club of families, the club of hope where the meek shall inherit the earth. (*Pause.*) That's what's on the video. The moment Watford died a thousand deaths.

The bell rings.

Why don't you get the door?

Dan Good idea.

Blackout.

SCENE TWO

*Bill, Shaun, Tim. Tim looks like a young Elton John,
down to the large pink-framed glasses.*

Bill Get my brother.

Shaun Why?

Bill Where is he?

Shaun He's on the phone.

Bill Get him now.

Shaun Keep your hair on.

Bill Don't tell me in my own house to keep my hair on.
It's my business whether I keep my hair on or throw it
around the room, all right?

Shaun Not much else to throw around is there?

Bill What did you say?

Shaun Talk about having a vacancy. Ha ha.

Bill (*to Tim*) Who are you?

Shaun Bed linen provided. But not the bed. Ha ha ha ha.

Bill I asked you a question.

Shaun Old Ghandi would feel a bit desolate in here.

Bill What did you say?

Shaun Mind if I have a sit down? Now where to go . . .

Bill picks up his chair as Shaun tries to sit in it.

Bill Get away from my chair! No one touches my chair.

Shaun All right, leave it out.

Bill No one sits in my chair. (*to Tim*) Don't look at me. Who are you? Don't look at me.

Enter Dan. Dan holds a mobile phone and finishes his conversation. Bill holds the chair.

Dan We should be with you around twelve. Looking forward to it. Yup. (*Sees them.*) Listen, got to go, Terry. Little something to clear up. Yup. See you Monday.

Bill Where've you been?

Dan I was calling Bristol. Is there a problem?

Bill Is this some kind of a joke?

Dan What?

Bill Tell him to take them off.

Dan This is Tim.

Bill Just tell him to take them off.

Dan Take what off?

Bill You are one sick human being.

Shaun Oy, listen.

Dan Shut it. (*to Bill*) I don't get it.

Bill He's wearing the glasses.

Dan He's short-sighted. He's very short-sighted. Aren't you, Tim?

Bill But he's not wearing any old glasses. He's wearing the glasses!

Dan What glasses?

Bill What glasses! What glasses?!

Pause.

Dan Oh, those glasses. (*explaining to the others*) Elton John's glasses.

Shaun You what?

Bill I was just getting over it. I was just making progress at forgetting, I mean do you understand what happens to a man who puts all his faith, all his love into something, I mean all of it so that he's got none left, and then it's all thrown back at him? It empties him out, and he's just managing to rediscover the slightest signs of life in his empty frame when he has to suffer the ignominy of having some squirt deliberately taking the piss out of him by wearing the same glasses!

Dan He's got to see to play the drums, Bill.

Bill But I mean deliberately rubbing the bitterest salt into his gaping bloody wounds by wearing the very same glasses!

Shaun What is he on?

Dan Bill, he didn't know. I'm sorry, it's my fault.

Bill I just don't know if I can let you stay. I mean, it's more than just a misunderstanding, I see it very much as a snub, yup, a snub to my hospitality. You know perfectly well I'm of a sensitive disposition at the moment but is there a glimmer of concern, oh no. No, I'm sorry. There are plenty of B&Bs or there's the hotel on the bypass since you're all so flush.

Dan No, Bill!

Bill Sorry, lads. Nothing personal. I probably should never have said yes in the first place. I got carried away, got a bit overexcited at the idea of seeing my little brother after all this time. I mean, just the slightest thing, you can see, although it's pretty bloody rich of you, but nevertheless I appreciate it must seem a bit O. T. T. from your angle.

Dan Listen, Bill, we can't stay in a B&B.

Bill Go to a hotel, you got money . . .

Dan No . . .

Bill . . . you don't need me, a slick operation like your-selves.

Dan But, Bill . . .

Bill No, I'm sorry, I've made up my mind.

Dan Bill, listen! I didn't come to Watford because I needed somewhere to fucking stay. Hardly on the way is it? On the way from Tranmere to Bristol? Had you thought of that?

Pause.

Bill Why'd you come then?

Dan I came here to see you! I haven't seen you for, well, for a long time, like we said. I don't want to go now.

Bill You came to see me?

Dan Yeah, I was worried, no, well, I was, let's say, curi-ous about your welfare, about how you were faring.

Bill About me?

Dan I know I haven't kept in touch much, but you're still very much on my mind. But I can't leave him. I'm like a father to him, you understand. Like you were to me.

Bill Listen, Dan, I really appreciate you taking an interest.

Dan I'm your little brother.

Bill I just can't do it. I can't look at them.

Dan He won't wear them in your presence.

Shaun Dan, he can't see a bloody thing! He'll hurt him-self.

Dan I'll look after him. It's only a weekend. OK. Tim? Tim?

Tim OK.

Bill No specs?

Dan No specs. He's not going anywhere, is he?

Bill I don't know. He's bound to put them on to do his teeth, and I'll walk into the bathroom.

Dan I'll do his teeth. I'll do his teeth for him.

Bill If I see him with them I'll go funny, I know I will.

Dan Take them off, Tim . . .

Tim does.

There you are. All right now?

Bill Better. Better. Still, the resemblance is uncanny.

Shaun Do you want him to have plastic surgery, just for the weekend?

Bill I'm beginning not to like you overly. What do you do?

Shaun I play bass.

Bill Figures.

Shaun And I drive the van.

Bill Renaissance Man. (*Pause.*) You can stay. Just for the weekend. And I'd prefer not to see him (*Tim*) and not to hear him (*Shaun*). That's ideally. It's good to see you, Dan.

Dan It's good to be back.

Bill Did you miss it?

Dan What, Watford? Yeah, yeah, yeah, yeah, I did.

Bill I bet you did. Show them round you should. Renaissance Man over there, you been here before?

Shaun Nah.

Bill What about Elton?

Shaun His name's Tim.

Bill Elton? What do you think of Watford?

Shaun He can't see it thanks to you.

Tim It's OK.

Bill Is that all? OK?

Shaun Well, it's hardly Florence, is it?

Dan Shaun!

Bill What do you mean it's hardly Florence? Been to Florence have you?

Shaun Nah.

Bill Well, I suggest you do before making sweeping statements like that. What's Florence got that Watford hasn't got? Nothing. Look out the window. You, Renaissance Man. Go on. Can you see it?

Shaun See what?

Bill The cathedral.

Shaun All I can see is a row of terraced housing.

Bill You're not looking properly! Look again. You see it now? The four spires over the top of the houses? At night they glow in the darkness. That's the cathedral. And people sing in it just like in any cathedral in Florence except in this cathedral they don't sing 'Hallelujah, Lord my shepherd, ding dong merrily on high', no, they sing, 'Who's the wanker, who's the wanker, who's the wanker in the black?' But it's a beautiful sound. And in this cathedral, instead of hymn books there are programmes and instead of a pulpit there's a dugout, and instead of a sermon on the mount and a loaf of bread feeding the five thousand, there's a half-time talk with a plate of oranges and a cup of Bovril. But this cathedral has real gods, and all over this beautiful town there are thousands of people worshipping those gods in little shrines. You want to see my shrine?

Dan Go on, Shaun.

Shaun Why?

Dan You like football.

Shaun No I don't. I hate it.

Dan Shaun!

Shaun Where is it?

Bill This way.

Dan Bill's inviting you into his cellar, Shaun. I hope you're not ungrateful.

Shaun Why me? Why is it always me?

Exeunt. Dan sits down, exhausted. After a while . . .

Tim Dan?

Dan Hold on, I'm thinking.

Pause.

Tim Dan?

Dan What?!

Tim Is it all over?

Dan Is what all over?

Tim The band.

Dan No, no, no. We're just in a temporary dip, that's all. We've had a run of bad luck.

Tim We lost all the instruments.

Dan I know.

Tim The venue manager in Tranmere took them. He locked them in his back room and told us to get lost. He took my drums.

Dan He was just disappointed that our gig hadn't gone as well as anticipated.

Tim We'll never hit the big time if we don't have any instruments.

Dan We'll find some more instruments.

Tim We haven't got any money.

Dan Well, we'll find some more money.

Tim The venue manager in Tranmere took the instruments because we didn't have the money we'd promised for the hire of the venue.

Dan Yeah, that was a miscalculation on my part, I estimated that our income from box office would cover the hire. Which it didn't quite do.

Tim Has Josette left for good?

Dan No, no, Josette just got a bit down like we all get down every now and then, and she said some things in haste and anger that she'll regret saying in the cool light of day. She'll come back.

Tim She was really angry.

Dan Yes she was.

Tim She spat in your face.

Dan Yes she did.

Tim She slapped Shaun and called him the worst musician she had ever met.

Dan Yes, I *was* there.

Tim She said she wasn't coming back.

Dan Yes, we all say things. I myself have said some things and could say so many more things. The point is that we have all been working on this for four years, well, Shaun for two years after Barry left, but the rest of us for four years, and we're not going to throw all that away because of one miserable, tight-fisted venue manager in Tranmere who wouldn't spot a star if you put him in an observatory and pointed a fucking great telescope into the night sky!

Tim Barry's a session bassist in London now.

Dan (*he knows*) Is he?

Tim He's played on a number one track.

Dan Really? Well, I'm pleased for him.

Tim He was no better than us.

Dan Barry was very good.

Tim You were better. You were the best.

Dan We were all good. We still are all good.

Tim Your brother doesn't like me.

Dan Course he does.

Tim You said he'd give us a bed each. There's not one bed in the place.

Dan Well, we'll have to manage with what we've got, won't we?

Tim Why don't you tell your brother the truth?

Dan Never! My brother needs me right now, you saw what it meant to him, my being here. I'm not going to let him down. So you keep your mouth shut. Got it?

Tim Where will we go if he throws us out?

Dan He's not going to throw us out.

Tim Your parents are dead, mine have already put us up for a month and Shaun's lost track of his.

Dan He's not going to throw us out! All we need to do is stay nice and tight here for the weekend. Then on Monday we've got the gig in Bristol. It's going to change everything!

Tim With no instruments and no lead singer.

Dan We'll find some more instruments!

Tim Josette's gone for ever.

Dan She'll be back.

Tim She's gone to London to pursue a solo career.

Dan She will be back.

Tim She'll probably go and work with Barry.

Dan You know, you're a great fucking help in times of trouble, you really are.

Tim I can't see anything.

Dan Yeah, I'm sorry about that.

Tim I can't see a single thing.

Dan How was I supposed to know that in my absence my brother had turned into a Buddhist maniac with an Elton John hang-up?! I know as band manager I'm supposed to foresee all eventualities but that one escaped my attention. I am truly sorry, all right?

Tim Josette was beautiful.

Dan Josette was a stupid stuck-up bitch with a throat so full of fags she could barely breathe, let alone sing.

Tim We'll never see Josette again.

Dan I hope Josette gets lung cancer and dies live on *Top of the Pops*.

Tim I'm really sad, Dan.

Dan We've just got to get some instruments! If we can just get some instruments, Josette'll come back and we'll go to Bristol. I know we will!

Tim I'm really deep-down sad.

Dan Yeah, me too, Tim. Me too.

Enter Shaun.

Shaun I have just seen the most amazing thing.

Dan Shaun, come here, we're having a crisis meeting.

Shaun It's in the cellar. It's like a gold mine, like a huge sea of gold. Scarves, shirts, hats, pictures, scattered everywhere, on the walls, hung from the ceiling. And there are candles, gold candles which he lit so I could see. He just stood there with this little smile on his lips. Didn't say a word. I stayed for a bit and then I left him there. I need some air. There's this really strong musty smell everywhere. I think all the stuff's quite old. Makes you feel a bit faint. (*He opens the door and sniffs the cold air.*)

Dan Shaun, we're having a meeting!

Shaun You know what? There was one thing he didn't have. There was no ball.

Dan Shaun!

Shaun No ball at all.

Suddenly a football bounces through the door and rolls gently across the floor to a standstill. They look at it. A pause.
Enter Bill. He sees the ball.

Bill Will someone please tell me what that is?

Enter Amy. She is in full Watford kit (with tracksuit bottoms).

Amy Excuse me, can I have my ball back?

Bill Who let her in?

Dan No one.

Bill I leave you two minutes and I'm invaded.

Dan Listen, take your ball and go.

Amy collects her ball.

Amy Do you want to play?

Bill Play what?

Amy Football.

Bill Why do you think we'd be interested in football?

Amy You're men. All men like football.

23

Bill No, we don't. Dan, get her out of here.

Dan Listen, we don't want to play, all right?

Amy Why not?

Dan Why not?

Bill I've got a long-term injury.

Dan You heard him.

Amy How about you?

Dan Me?

Amy Thought we might have a game on the road.

Dan What makes you think I have got time for a little weekend kickaround with you? I'm the manager of a band! Did Brian Epstein play football with The Beatles? Did Malcolm McLaren play headers and volleys with The Sex Pistols?

Amy Who's Malcolm McLaren?

Dan Forget it.

Amy Are you a band?

Dan Yes, we are. And we're having a meeting.

Amy What are you called?

Dan We're called Goldilox.

Shaun With an 'x'.

Amy Never heard of you.

Dan You will. You will.

Amy I'm seeing Cusp tomorrow night. They're playing at the Colosseum. They're brilliant.

Dan (*trying to keep calm*) Are they really?

Amy Yeah. It's a sell-out.

Dan Is it?

Amy I've got two posters on my wall. One is of Luther Blissett of Watford and the other is of Travis Dickson of Cusp. He's the lead singer.

Dan Yes, I know. Anything else?

Amy What about him? Can he play (*Tim*)?

Dan You might find you'd have a problem with him.

Amy What?

Shaun He's gone temporarily blind.

Amy (*to Tim*) Hello.

Shaun She's talking to you, Tim.

Tim Oh. Hi.

Amy I'm Amy.

Tim I'm Tim.

Amy Hi, Tim.

Tim Hello, Amy.

  Pause.

Bill Who *are* you?

Amy I'm Amy. I live just round the corner.

Bill Well, I suggest you go back there before things turn nasty.

Amy What's wrong with you?

Bill Nothing.

Amy Then why ain't you got no furniture?

Dan suddenly worries for Amy's life.

Dan Look, Shaun, give her a quick game, will you?

Shaun Why me? Why is it always me?

Bill You're a Renaissance Man. Goes with the job.

Dan Go on, Shaun. (*to Amy*) He's good.

Shaun I'm not. I'm rubbish, you know I'm rubbish. She'll slaughter me.

Bill Exploit your size. Give her a kick early doors, that should put her in her place.

Dan She only wants a bit of fun. She's probably lonely. Look at her. She can't be more than fourteen.

Amy I'm sixteen.

Shaun I'm the worst player ever!

Amy Listen, forget it. I'll see you later.

Amy leaves VERY slowly. And sure enough . . .

Shaun All right! All right! I'll play. But only for ten minutes.

Amy Whatever.

Shaun One on one? Oh God, I haven't got a chance.

Bill Keep it tight at the back, you'll be fine.

Shaun Dan, at least go in goal. Help me out a bit.

Dan I've got things to do.

Tim I'll go in goal.

Dan How the fuck can you go in goal?

Tim I used to play in goal at school. If you give me the glasses back, I'll be fine.

Bill NO WAY! I knew that would happen. I turn my back for one second and it's all back where we started.

Amy I didn't mean to cause trouble.

Bill Well, that's funny because that's exactly what you have done. You waltz in here calm as you like, and within ten seconds a happy family atmosphere has been turned into civil war!

Dan Bill, she just wanted a game.

Bill If I see those glasses on him one more time . . .!

Dan He's not wearing the glasses, all right? Forget it, Tim. You're not playing. Go on, Shaun.

Shaun No, I'm sorry, but I demand that Tim should be allowed to play. I'm not playing unless Tim plays! (*He sits down on the floor.*)

Dan I don't believe this. Shaun, get up.

Shaun No, somebody's got to make a stand!

Dan Help me, God.

Shaun Ever since we arrived here we've been at the beck and call of your brother. Now I'm all for when in Rome do as the Romans, but when you're in Broadmoor someone's got to point out who are the nurses and who are the patients!!

   Confused pause.

Dan Bill, listen. What if they were to go and play and Tim was to put the glasses on outside the door. That wouldn't be a problem would it? I want to talk with you anyway.

Bill Suppose.

Dan Great. Everyone happy? Shaun, give Tim a hand

out. And knock before you come back in. Hold on, I've got the glasses.

> *He hands them over to Shaun. Outside, Tim crashes into a dustbin. The door closes. Bill puts on the video. It plays. Dan, uneasy, looks through the window.*

Come and have a look at this. She's keeping the ball up all the way along the road. Both feet. She's phenomenal. Would you look at that! (*He sees that Bill is not interested.*) Reminds me of when I used to watch you play for the school. It's funny, all the things I've forgotten in my life, for some reason I can still remember all the goals you scored. Like an action replay. You were so good. Yeah, well . . . What's wrong with the TV? The top half of the picture's all fuzzy.

Bill It's the VCR. It's suffering from over-use.

Dan But you can only see the players' legs.

Bill You get used to it.

Dan But how do you know who's who?

Bill From the shape of their calf muscle. I know all the Watford players' calves. Only thing is it's getting worse so soon I'll have to go on boot size and brand name alone.

Dan Why don't you get a new VCR?

Bill I'm not bothered.

Dan But, Bill, if you're watching it as much as you seem to . . .

Bill Well, the fact is I'm running a bit short at the moment. I expect you can't remember what that's like.

Dan How long's it been like that (*the video*)?

Bill Three, four months. Yeah, it's not ideal.

Dan (*looking at the screen*) Whose are those legs?

Bill Les Taylor. Midfield powerhouse. Missed a simple chance, third minute.

Dan And that?

Bill That's a balding, crooked loser.

Dan You can tell that from his ankles?

Bill It's the ref.

Dan Oh, I see. Whose are the red socks?

Bill Steve Sherwood.

Dan Oh, is this it? There he goes. His feet are in the air. And there are some blue feet in the air as well. What's happening? Oh, it's in. It's in the net. Look at the blue feet jumping up and down with all the other blue feet. The red feet are all standing dead still.

Was that it, Bill? Was that it?

Bill Yeah, that was it.

Dan I didn't see the flash of light. You know that flash of light off Elton John's glasses. Maybe I missed it. (*Pause.*) I'm sorry I didn't come before. I should have come.

Bill You've been busy building the band. If you're going to be a success then you've got to make sacrifices. If I was going to make a success out of myself I wouldn't stand on ceremony, and neither did you. I'm not ashamed to say I'm very proud of you, little brother. You're a credit to the family. Oh yes. I've told a lot of people about you.

Dan (*sadly*) What people, Bill?

Bill What do you mean, what people?

Dan I'm just wondering what people you see.

Bill Lots of people. Just people. Like that woman I told you about. The twenty-two-year-old.

Dan I'd like to meet her.

Bill Well, you can't. She's married. Got a kid. Yeah. Likes to keep me as her little secret. She comes here when they go and watch the football. Like this afternoon. So you can't. Impossible.

Dan Fine.

Bill Don't get me wrong. I appreciate you being here. Taking a detour just to see me. But my life is my life.

Dan Listen, Bill.

Bill What now?

Dan Nothing.

Bill Are you embarrassed by me?

Dan No, of course not.

Bill Because don't stay here on my account.

Dan I want to stay. You're my big brother!

Bill Am I?

Dan Of course you are! I just want to know what's happened, that's all.

Bill Nothing's happened!

Dan Looks like it.

Bill Nothing happened. Nothing happened.

Dan So why don't you go and play?

Bill I told you. Long-term injury.

Dan I just think maybe you could do with a bit of air.

Bill What do you mean?

Dan Well, look at you.

Bill Don't want it. Don't want to. No, I think I'll go downstairs. Give you some time to make plans.

Dan No, stay. I didn't mean to . . .

Bill Didn't mean to what?! Telling me I need to get some air! How old am I? You think I can't look after myself? What do you think I am?! You think I'm funny or something?! You think I'm a cripple?!

Dan I don't know what you are! I barely recognized you at first. You need to get out! You need to get going again!

Bill Don't tell me what I need! . . .

Dan I'm your brother . . .

Bill Don't ever tell me what I need!

Dan . . . I know what you were like!

Bill Well, you don't know any more! Six years away and you wander in and start acting like the Samaritans. I should be the one worried about you! You're going a bit funny in the head, mate! All that travelling's done you no good at all!

Dan You can't.

Bill What?

Dan You can't go out.

Bill Course I can.

Dan Go on then. Go and have a kickaround.

Bill I've got a long-term injury.

Dan Run it off.

Bill No, it's an internal injury, you can't, you can't just, it's not a case of just . . . running it off.

Dan When did you last step outside that door?

Bill I don't know. I mean, I do it all the time.

Dan Prove it. Step outside.

Bill Prove I can step outside my own door?

Dan Just do it. If it's that easy. Make me look a fool.

Bill I've never heard anything so stupid.

Dan Go on then. Show me what an idiot I am.

Bill I will. Now?

Very slowly he approaches the door. There is a tremendous strain in his movements, a terrific concentration. Finally he opens the door and takes a big breath but still doesn't go outside.

Dan Pop outside for a sec. Just to ram the point home.

Bill pops out and back again.

Bill There you are. No problem.

Dan One more time?

Bill steps out again. This time he returns a little later. And calmer.

Bill The sky's so high, isn't it?

Dan Is it?

Bill Nice day though.

Dan Good day for a kickaround.

Bill You know what? Maybe I might have a little kickaround after all. If that's all right with you?

Dan Sure. You want me to come?

Bill No. No. I'll be fine. You know I haven't touched a ball in six years?

Dan Pretty much when I left.

Bill Yeah. Right, see you later then. (*He goes to leave.*) What about the glasses? He's wearing the glasses.

Dan Look at his knees. Like on the video. You can do that.

Bill Dan. I can.

Bill leaves and closes the door. Dan heaves a deep sigh. Blackout.

SCENE THREE

Dan and Shaun.

Dan Where are they? They've been over three hours!

Shaun Your brother's really got back into the habit. I mean, as a person I think he's unbelievably sad, but I've got to give it to him on the football pitch. He's dead good. And fit. 180 minutes of non-stop football after a long lay-off. No sign of the injury.

Dan Really.

Shaun Mind you, she's still the best. When I left she was beating him. Although I reckon Tim's been letting her shots in on purpose. Because he's just about saved every-thing your brother's throwing at him, and I never even scored once. Not once in a whole afternoon. Whereas she's scored over forty times.

Dan Why's he letting her score?

Shaun Why do you think? It's because he's sweet for her, isn't he?

Dan Tim?

Shaun Yeah. When he put on the glasses to play goalie, he just stopped and stared at her for ages. And then, whenever she scores, he claps and cheers. You're not supposed to do that if you're the opposition goalie! You're supposed to curse and hold your head in your hands. But not Tim.

Dan Tim's never been near a woman.

Shaun And then he goes and gets the ball from a car park, or a nearby garden, and once even from a river, yeah, he waded in to get it, it must have been bloody freezing, and he comes back and deliberately kicks it back to her. And to be honest, when I left your brother was getting just a bit wound up about it, about Tim's bias I mean.

Dan Well, if they're not back soon you'll have to go and get him. We need him for this afternoon.

Shaun What's the plan, Dan?

Dan Shaun, what are we lacking that would make us a really great band?

Shaun Uh, the killer touch?

Dan Think simple, Shaun.

Shaun I don't know.

Dan What's in the van, Shaun?

Shaun Fuck all right now.

Dan Exactly. I'll tell you what we are lacking. We are lacking everything that we need to become a great band. Everything. You hear me? We are lacking a singer, we are lacking instruments to play the songs that the hypothetical singer might then sing at the gig at which the hypothetical songs could then be sung. Shaun, we can sum up our situation in one word. Crisis. And you do not seem to be able to do anything but to be thrashed at football by a lonely teenage girl and to antagonize my brother who is the one person in the world willing to offer us a sodding roof over our sodding heads!

Shaun Oh yeah? And who's the one who drives the van, and who's the one who parks the van, and who's the one who loads and unloads the gear . . .

Dan (*over the top of him*) What gear? What gear? What fucking gear?!

Shaun . . . whilst you and that bitch sit around smoking and giggling together like a couple of lovebirds? Who does all that? Me. I do!

Dan Who introduced you to me, Shaun?

Shaun I don't know. (*He does.*)

Dan Your mother. You came to see a gig of ours with your mother. She was the only pensioner in the audience. You were a thirty-year-old living in a two up two down with your mother. It was your mother who told me you played bass. She sold you to me and then she moved away but she didn't tell you where she went. She wanted you to leave, Shaun. She must have been the only mother tied to the apron strings of her son. Goldilox is your last chance, Shaun.

Pause.

Shaun So, what's the plan?

Dan I need you to find me a VCR. It doesn't have to be new. It just has to work.

Shaun Why?

Dan If you find me a VCR, I promise I will have for you this very evening a brand-new bass guitar.

Shaun How?

Dan Trust me, Shaun.

Shaun I love this band, Dan. I'd do anything for this band.

Persistent ringing at the door.

Dan About time.

He opens the door. Bill is being carried and is breathing very heavily.

Bill Ow! Watch it!

Dan What's wrong?

Bill What kind of a stupid question's . . .?

Tim Help me, I can't see anything.

Amy Straight on. Almost there.

Bill It's ligaments. I can tell.

Dan How did he do it? What's happened to you?

Tim It was a late challenge. He slid in on me.

Bill Bollocks I did. It was a totally fair tackle, just mis-timed it a bit on the hard ground.

Amy More than a bit.

Bill Yeah well, we can have the post-match discussion later. In the meantime, are we going to stand here all day or do you think that amongst you you could find me somewhere a bit more comfortable? That chair looks worth a try.

Dan I can't believe this.

Amy This is going to hurt.

Bill Just get me in it. AAAAH!

Amy That's it.

Bill Oh God, it's ligaments, never felt so much pain, I'll be out for months.

Shaun Hold the back page.

Bill Still, I don't regret a single moment. Wonderful!

Shaun Who won?

Tim Amy. Amy won.

Bill Amy was winning. But I was making a sensational comeback when we had to stop. Thirty-three twenty-seven it was. I'd just scored three in a row, all low rasping drives past Elton there. And then I went past Amy as if she wasn't there but played it a bit too far ahead of me. It was a fifty-fifty ball. I had to go for it.

Tim I had the ball in my hands!

Bill Always a difficult one to call.

Tim You clattered right into me. Like you really meant me some harm.

Bill Just a bit of honest aggression.

Tim And you broke my glasses. You smashed them. Look at them.

Dan Oh no.

Shaun That's it. I've had enough. You are a mad, deranged, dangerous . . .

Dan Shaun, shouldn't you be going somewhere? Shaun?

Exit Shaun.

Tim They're special lenses, Dan. How am I going to see?

Dan It was supposed to be a weekend kickaround!

Amy Things got a bit tense as Bill made his comeback.

Bill I'd just begun to rediscover the old touch. At first I found myself a little behind the play. But I was starting to flow when the accident happened.

Tim He used foul language.

Bill I did not.

Tim He called Amy a cheating little . . .

Bill I did not!

Tim You said you'd make it so she'd never walk again.

Bill All spoken in the heat of battle.

Tim And he kept calling me Elton and saying how this time I wasn't going to deny him.

Dan How bad is it?

Bill Bad.

Dan Shall I call an ambulance?

Bill I'm not going anywhere. I'll heal here.

Amy I'll look after him.

Dan Perfect. Leave Amy to it. We've got work to do.

Tim What work?

Dan Band business. Anyway, Bill's got a kind of meeting.

Bill Oh Christ, I forgot about that.

Dan What time does the meeting end?

Bill Full-time. Ten to five.

Dan We'll be back at five. Let's go.

Tim Where are we going?

Dan Follow me.

Tim I can't see you.

Dan Hold my hand.

Tim Amy. Where are you?

Amy Here, Tim. I'm here.

Tim I'll be back soon.

Exeunt.

Bill That's better. Bit of peace. Such a noisy business having visitors.

Amy You shouldn't get so worked up.

Bill Got a bit pissed off that he was deliberately letting in all those goals of yours. Did you notice that?

Amy Don't know. Maybe he did.

Bill Course he did. Watford supporter are you?

Amy Yeah. I go to every home game.

Bill Going today?

Amy Do you want to come?

Bill No, thanks for the offer. I've got this meeting. We're not doing so well now are we?

Amy If we lose today we go down.

Bill So I heard. I can hear through the window you see. I know all the sounds, what they mean. Whether it's goal for us or for them, or a disallowed goal, a corner, or a dodgy off-side. And the final whistle, whether we've won or whether we've lost. Mostly we've lost recently. Is that right?

Amy Why don't you go to the games?

Bill Well, it's because I felt really let down after the F. A. Cup Final of 1984. Maybe you don't remember it.

Amy I was there.

Bill You were there? I was there!

Amy My dad took me.

Bill Well then, you'll understand!

Amy I was four.

Bill Oh, right. Was it that long ago?

Amy Come with me.

Bill Go with your boyfriend.

Amy I don't want a boyfriend.

Bill Why not? You should have loads of boyfriends by now, being nice-looking like you are, and good at football. That's some combination.

Amy I'm not pretty enough.

Bill Of course you are. Who told you that? You've got a nice little nose, sparky little eyes, nice tall athletic body; bit of make-up, bit of a hair-do and you could be all right. Bit of a bob or something. (*Pause.*) Go with your dad.

Amy He's not around. He used to take me all the time when I was young. He was fanatical. He knew all the players, knew some of them really well. He knew Luther Blissett.

Bill Really?

Amy Yeah. But then when I was ten him and mum . . . well, it didn't work out. He lives in Aberdeen now. He's working on an oil rig. I still write to him. I write him reports of the games. Yeah. I want to be a reporter. Like in the newspapers?

Bill You should be a player.

Amy I'm too small.

Bill Rubbish.

Amy I'm too easily knocked off the ball. And I'm getting . . .

Bill What?

Amy Well, I'm developing . . . (*She indicates her breasts.*)

Bill No, I don't agree. I mean, not that you're not developing. I'm sure you are. No, I mean, you should trial.

Amy I'm happy writing. I've done it every game for five years.

Bill That's a lot of games.

Amy One hundred and thirty. When I started I was only ten so they were a bit simple. Like, 'We won and were brilliant,' and that was it. But I'm good now.

Bill I'd like to read one.

Amy Well, you can't, they're just for him. (*Pause.*) Bill.

Bill What?

Amy Who are you meeting?

Bill What? Oh, no one.

Amy It's not a woman is it?

Bill No, what makes you think that?

Amy I've seen that look before.

Bill Look like what?

Amy A look like you're really interested in everything, like if I was talking about physics you'd be going, 'oh really, that's interesting', and bending your eyebrows, because all you're thinking about is some woman.

Bill No, God no.

Amy I mean, are you really interested in talking to me?

Bill Of course I am.

Amy I really hated it when he did that. Lied to me.

Bill Who?

Amy My dad.

Bill No, no, there's no woman.

Amy Promise?

Bill Promise. Promise.

Amy Yeah, well anyway, what time is it?

Bill Twenty-to.

Amy Can I use your bathroom? I won't be long.

Bill Take your time. They won't be here until three.

Amy enters the bathroom.

They're very punctual business people.

The bell rings. Bill stands up in shock. A key in the lock. The door opens. Julie enters with bags of shopping, a white sheet, and a bottle of wine.

Bill You're early!

Julie Last game of the season. Don't want to miss it.

Bill I'm not ready!

Julie You look ready enough for me. (*She kisses him. She presents a bottle and goes to sort out the shopping.*) Slovenia. God knows. I've brought your weekly provisions. Got you some salad. Can't live on takeaway deliveries for ever. What've you done to your leg?

Bill I fell over. Fell over the chair.

Julie Quite an achievement in this place.

Bill What are you doing here?

Julie They went early to get good seats at the game. Full house apparently.

Bill Yeah, well, I like to keep to a schedule. Can you come back in ten minutes?

Julie Don't be daft. (*She picks up Tim's broken glasses.*) Whose are these?

Bill Those? Mine.

Julie You're not short-sighted.

Bill I used to be. (*He takes the glasses and puts them in the drawer.*)

Julie Are you all right?

Bill Fine.

Julie Last game of the season. What you going to do without me?

Bill Listen, Julie.

Julie Big game today isn't it? If we lose, we go down.

Bill Yes, I know.

Julie (*finds corkscrew*) Big crowd, that's what I like. I

43

remember, not long after we started seeing each other, when they had a full house. The windows shook. And you opened them up and there we were with the roar of the crowd ringing around us. Haven't had that kind of sound for a while, Bill, have we?

Bill Julie, I feel a bit unwell.

Julie You don't look it.

Bill Don't I?

Julie No. There's a colour in your face.

Bill Probably just the light.

Julie There have been times when I thought you were glued to that chair. But today you look as if you could explode at any second.

Bill Really.

Julie Maybe it's the excitement's making you dizzy.

Bill I don't think so.

Julie Want some wine?

Bill No thank you.

Julie Slovenia? Where is that? (*She stubs out her cigarette and removes her top.*)

Bill What are you doing?

Julie What does it look like I'm doing?

Bill No, put it back on again.

Julie It's a big game, I want to be ready for kick-off. I want to take advantage of the extra warm-up time.

Bill Listen, can't we talk first?

Julie Forty-five minutes each way may be enough for you, but I need a little more. I'm a slow starter.

Bill Julie, I'm not in the mood.

Julie What?

Bill I think I'm ill.

Julie Headache?

Bill No, maybe it's the leg. Put it back on.

Julie Where does it hurt? Have you soaked it? (*Heads for bathroom.*)

Bill No!! (*He leaps up, immediately falls over again in agony.*) Aah! It's ligaments, very complicated. Listen, can't we leave it just a week?

Julie You know perfectly well we can't. It's the last game of the season.

Bill There's next season.

Julie Bill, you're a bit like a cigarette. I need you at very precise times. Maybe I'm an unusually addictive person. Anyway, with you, it's once a week. I have to have you once a week, you see? It's like the cigarette, I don't want to need you, but I absolutely do. It's like being a fan. I'm a fan of you, Bill. Nothing I can do. Frightening, isn't it?

Bill Well, come back and be a fan in half an hour. I'm just not ready right now!

Julie I don't think I can wait. You're firing me up today. There's an energy coming off you.

Bill It's not that kind of energy! Can't we just go for a walk?

Pause.

Julie You? Go for a walk?

Bill Yeah.

Julie Who is she?

Bill What?

Julie The girl in the bathroom.

Bill No one. There's no one.

Julie I shouldn't have come early. I didn't know you scheduled us so tightly. You're more organized than I gave you credit for. But I'm here now, it seems a bit prudish to leave and come back just for the sake of decorum.

Bill No, you've got it completely wrong.

Julie I know that face, Bill. I've seen it before.

Bill What? What is going on? There is no one in there.

The loo flushes.

OK, there is someone. But not that kind of someone. You have to believe me.

Julie Enjoy the match.

Bill No, wait. No, wait, you have to meet her, because it's not what you think. We played football together, that's all.

Julie And she's taking a post-match shower?

Bill Yes! Kind of. We played football and that's where this colour you keep going on about has come from. I'm cold and I'm knackered and I did my leg in.

Julie You played football outside?

Bill Yeah.

Julie Bill, I have spent all year trying to get you to take two steps outside this door. And now you'd have me believe that you casually wander off for an afternoon's healthy exercise whenever the opportunity arises. If you fucked someone else, you fucked someone else. But don't lie to me.

Bill Sshhh! I'm not lying. You'll understand when you see her.

Julie I thought you didn't want me to see her.

Bill No, I didn't want her to see you!

Julie Oh, thanks.

Bill No, but now I do, now I absolutely do.

Julie Of course. I'm an embarrassment to you.

Bill Of course you're not.

Julie Listen, forget it.

Bill Wait! Amy! Amy! Come out.

Julie What did you say?

Bill Amy! Come on out. It's all fine, it's all been cleared up.

Julie No, Bill. Wait.

Bill Come on!

Julie No, Bill, Bill!

The door opens. It is Amy with full Watford war-paint on her face, a bright orange with 'Hornets' in black on the top. Julie freezes.

Bill Amy, this is Julie, my girlfriend.

Pause.

Amy Hello Mum.

Blackout.

Act Two

Bill and Julie. In the background the slight sound of a football crowd. One wine bottle empty on the ground. Another half drunk. Julie depressed, Bill frustrated.

Bill Listen to that! We haven't had a full house for months.

Julie I'm just not in the mood. OK?

Bill You were desperate for a sound like that!

Julie But now I'm not.

Bill You were.

Julie And you weren't, all right?

Bill That's because I had your daughter in the bathroom. Where are you going?

Julie To kill myself.

Bill Let's go to bed first.

Julie What's got into you?

Bill I don't know, big crowd, last game, you all emotional, it just gets a man aroused.

Julie How will I look at her? She didn't say a word. Just walked straight out the door.

Bill She had to get to the game!

Julie She'll run away. She'll run away to her father.

Bill No, all she needs is a win. The flush of victory will cast a rosy hue over the whole affair.

Julie I lied to her, to my own daughter. I hate her! How did that . . . that sweet, unsoiled face come out of me?

Bill I like her.

Julie Fancy them young do you?

Bill I didn't mean that.

Julie Sure you didn't.

Bill You need a top up.

Julie You're trying to get me drunk.

Bill Rubbish.

Julie Well, it won't work. I just get sadder with each glass. And you get uglier.

Bill A full house! At long last a full house, and all I'm getting is insults and abuse!

Julie Will you shut up about your full house! God, you disgust me.

Bill Oh, thank you.

Julie You are a disgusting, deceitful piece of filth, you really are.

Bill But I care about you.

Julie You! You don't care about me.

Bill Of course I do!

Julie I come in here and undress and drink red wine like a whore and meanwhile my daughter is in the bathroom and you don't say a bloody thing! Is that caring?!

Bill I didn't know, did I!

Julie All you needed to say was 'she's in the bathroom'.

Bill I didn't know she was in the bathroom!

Julie I would have left. (*Hears what he said.*) What do you mean, you didn't know? Of course you knew!

Bill I mean I didn't know *she* was in the bathroom. I didn't know who she was, did I?

Julie None of this would have happened if you hadn't lied to me.

Bill I lied?

Julie You're such a coward. That's what I can't stand.

Bill *I* lied?

Julie Yes, you!

Bill And how's the husband? You know, the faithful, ignorant man at home you told me about.

Julie Bill, shut up.

Bill No, you remember the one, the one who 'mustn't know'! . . .

Julie I said that's enough!

Bill . . . Who must never ever know! The one who'd axe me to death if he found out about us . . . I don't know why you were so worried, I mean, not much chance of him knowing anything when he's fucked off to live in Aberdeen, is there?

Julie Well, at least he could buy his own shopping!

A sudden roar then a groan of disappointment. They freeze.

Near miss.

Bill Tipped over the bar I imagine.

Julie Oh, Bill.

Bill Please. Julie. Listen to it.

Julie Why today? Why not last week? Last week there were three men and a dog and now I'm in a Greek tragedy and it's like the Mardi Gras out there. (*She downs another glass.*) It's her birthday, Bill. It's Amy's sixteenth birthday today.

Bill Oh.

Julie My daughter becomes a woman today, and she's going on her own to a football match, then she's going on her own to the Cusp concert at the Colosseum. She's a lonely girl who thinks she's Jimmy Hill and now on top of all that she has a whore for a mother who lies to her at every opportunity.

Bill I'm sorry.

Julie I'm going to the shop to get another bottle.

Bill No, I'll go.

Julie You?

Bill Yeah, I'll go.

Julie You don't go anywhere.

Bill No, I want to go. You're always doing everything. I'll go this time.

Julie What's happened to you?

Bill Slovenia! (*He turns back.*) Why didn't you tell me?

Julie I don't know. It was easier. I was going to tell you. I don't know. Just get the wine, OK . . .

Bill Yeah. (*He moves to go.*)

Julie It'll be a new experience seeing you coming through that door.

Bill Yeah.

Julie Go on then. I'll be ready for you when you get back.

Bill You will?

Julie Last game of the season. Don't want to waste it do we?

A distant whistle and a sound from the crowd.

Half-time. You got fifteen minutes.

Bill rushes out. Julie goes into the bathroom. She comes out with her skirt off, starts to unfold the sheet, stops.

What am I doing?

The bell rings urgently. Julie goes only after the persistence of the ring. She opens. It is Dan. He piles into the room carrying one lead guitar and one bass guitar. Julie fetches her skirt.

Who the hell are you?

Dan I'm Bill's brother. Can I come in? (*He enters pulling lots of musical gear. During the conversation, he gets it all inside.*)

Julie Bill hasn't got a brother.

Dan He has. I'm him. I've been away. Nice to meet you.

Julie He said he was an only son.

Dan He said you were twenty-two.

Julie You know who I am?

Dan Well, I think I know what you are.

Julie What do you mean, what I am?

Dan Sorry, it came out wrong.

Julie He said I was twenty-two?

Dan But you are . . .? I mean, you are who . . . you are who I think . . . It's just he said you were twenty-two.

Julie Uh huh.

Dan Yeah . . . and platinum blonde, with legs like . . .

Julie Like what?

Dan I'm Dan. I'm a manager of a band. We're just on our way through. These are our instruments.

Pause. Julie is staring at Dan.

What? What? What?

Julie . . .

Dan Sorry?

Julie . . .

Dan What? What?

Julie (*in despair*) . . .

Dan I know you.

Julie Tenby.

Dan Tenby.

Julie Two years ago.

Dan The Sapphire. We played there. We played like shit. I got heavily involved with a bottle of tequila . . . (*Pause. He remembers.*) No. That wasn't you. No, she was different. Oh God. No. You're not . . . her. Oh God.

Julie You're his brother. Oh God.

Dan Oh God. You looked different.

Julie You had long hair.

Dan I was unhappy.

Julie Not as unhappy as I was.

Dan Oh God. I'm sorry.

Julie I went to the saddest, most sordid nightspot on earth and pulled the lead guitarist of a band from nowhere.

Dan You said we were brilliant.

Julie 'Oh, you were . . .'

Dan And then we . . .

Julie Up against a sea wall. It was pissing down. In July.

Dan Oh God. Can I?

Julie gives him a cigarette. They smoke together.

Julie We mustn't tell him.

Dan No.

Julie I hate myself.

Dan Listen . . .

Julie Julie.

Dan Yeah, Julie, listen, did we manage to . . .

Julie No, not really. Half. Ish.

Dan No, I thought not.

Julie Don't lose sleep over it.

Dan But after we'd done it, half, ish, didn't we both . . . well, cry a lot? Did I make that up? I cried first. Don't know why. That seemed to get you going. But you wouldn't stop. You kept shaking. I kept trying to hold you.

Julie I think it was the sound of the sea.

Dan I just remember holding you, and saying shut up, you stupid bitch, and then holding you again. And you were sick on my jacket!

Julie You were very nice about it.

Dan I just didn't notice 'til the morning.

Julie And then we arranged to meet the next day in a cafe.

Dan (*guiltily*) Did we?

Julie Don't worry, I didn't turn up either.

Dan And now you're here seeing . . . how did you two . . . oh God, this is terrible.

Julie Met him when I got back. He was wandering along the road with his groceries and he looked terrible. I thought he was choking, he looked all dizzy. Anyway, I got him back here. Two bottles of wine later and we were sleeping with each other. What was I like?

Dan And now you're together?

Julie Not really. It's once a week. I bring him provisions. He's not been able to go out.

Dan I'd gathered.

Julie Well, you've obviously changed him, look at him now. Rushing all over the place.

Dan And you?

Julie I don't know. Bill's been good for me. When you and I had our . . . I'd been alone for a while. I wasn't that well.

Dan You look much better.

Julie You mean I look less of a blur . . . No, so do you. Nice guitars.

Dan What about them?

Julie Looks like Travis Dickson's. From Cusp? My daughter's a big fan. Got posters all over the bedroom.

Dan Yeah, listen, when will Bill be back?

Julie Any minute.

Dan Couldn't give me a hand getting this stuff in the bathroom could you? I don't want it to be seen from the window. There's nothing wrong! It's just it's valuable you see.

Dan goes to the bathroom with guitars. Dan puts guitars in bathroom. Julie picks up the hi-hat. Dan comes out of the bathroom. They meet.

Julie In Tenby. I think you saved my life.

They kiss suddenly, passionately. The cymbal crashes to the floor. Dan breaks off.

Dan No, stop.

Julie Yeah, absolutely.

Dan I don't have room for this.

Julie No, nor do I.

Dan And it would kill Bill. It would kill him.

Julie Yeah, absolutely.

Dan I should go. I'll just put these in the bathroom . . . tell him I dropped them off.

Julie Of course.

Dan Right.

Julie takes the hi-hat into the bathroom. Dan picks up the two amplifiers and goes into bathroom.

Empty stage. We hear the sound of a cymbal crashing in the bathroom once more.

The whistle for the start of the second half blows. Enter Bill with wine. He is breathing hard from a slight panic attack and the effort of hobbling fast. He slams the door behind him.

Bill Julie?

Enter Julie hurriedly from the bathroom.

Julie Bill, what you doing here?

Bill I live here.

Julie You were so quick.

Bill Ran, didn't I?

Julie Thought you were injured.

Bill Ran it off. Best way. Thought you were getting ready for me.

Julie I was.

Bill I've just heard the strangest thing. This panda car stops me as I'm jogging along minding my business and this copper asks me if I've seen a man running around with a load of musical instruments. Apparently, Cusp have had their gear nicked. Would you believe that? Two thousand kids going to that gig tonight, your Amy included, and some selfish little twat steals their gear. Some people. (*He heads bathroomwards.*)

Julie Where are you going?

Bill Get the condoms.

Julie No, I'll go.

She kisses him and goes into the bathroom. Bill unrolls the sheet on the mattress and prepares himself. In the crowd there is a rising roar but then a groan.

Bill Missed it. Easy chance. Craig Rammage at a guess. (*to Julie*) Can't you find them?

Julie comes immediately out of the bathroom with a packet of Durex and a towel.

Julie Bill? Have you ever thought of doing it differently?

Bill What have you got in mind?

Julie I want to blindfold you, Bill. It will be just you and me and the roar of the crowd.

Pause.

Bill What with?

Julie I could only find this towel.

Bill Not so sure about that. It's a bit of a health risk, to be honest.

Julie Well, what else have you got?

Bill Only a sock.

Julie A sock.

Bill No, I've got it! I've got just the thing.

He goes out into the cellar. Julie goes to the bathroom, talks into it.

Julie Quick!

Dan pelts from the bathroom but is stopped in mid-run.

Bill (*from cellar*) Yes!

Julie waves Dan back into the bathroom as Bill

returns with a Watford scarf from 1984.

1984 Cup Final. The very one I wore.

Julie Come here. (*She ties it around his eyes.*) What can you see?

Bill The entire Watford line-up, 1984. John Barnes. Les Taylor. George Reilly.

Julie Enjoy the game.

They kiss. Then Dan creeps out of the bathroom. Julie waves him silently towards the door. He is half-way across when Bill speaks and Dan freezes.

Bill Julie.

Julie Quiet, Bill.

Bill No, I want you to know something. I want you to know about Dan. The fact is that I've lied to you too. I told you I had no relatives. I do. I have a little brother called Dan.

Julie Tell me later, Bill.

Bill gets up. As he talks he undoes the blindfold, but still does not see Dan, who is right behind him.

Bill No, you see Dan's come back. He's been away managing this rock band but he's come back specially to visit me. I never told you about him because . . . well, because he's so successful with the band and I had this idea you'd become more interested in him, you see.

Julie How could you think that?

Bill throws the scarf over his shoulders but leaves it over Dan's, who is still right behind him.

Bill He's going to be massive, he's big already, but he's going to be massive. When I was young I always thought I was the talented one and that he was a loser, but it's the other way around. I'm a nobody who doesn't even buy his own meals, he's on the verge of stardom. Well, anyway, I want you to meet him.

Julie grabs the scarf.

Julie Great. Put your blindfold on, Bill.

Bill Stay after the game. No secrets any more, Julie. Say you'll stay. Promise.

Julie Promise.

Happy, Bill returns the blindfold and they kiss again. Dan, relieved, heads towards the door and very quietly opens it. But on the other side he finds Shaun listening in with his ear to the door.

Dan Aah!

Chaos. Bill and Julie leap up. Bill removes the blindfold. Shaun looks on in confusion.

Shaun This is weird.

Bill What time do you call this? I said ten to five.

Shaun I think I should go.

Dan You're not going anywhere, Shaun.

Shaun No, but this is pretty weird.

Bill Will somebody answer my question?!

Dan We've got a present for you, Bill. Shaun and I have come round with a surprise present.

Shaun We what?

Bill How did you get in?

Dan The door was open, wasn't it, Shaun?

Shaun What?

Dan I said the door was open so on our way back from getting Bill his present, we just opened it.

Bill I closed the door!

Dan No, Bill, it was open. I mean, how else could we have got in?

Bill Julie, I closed the door!

Julie No, Bill, I don't think so.

Bill I closed the door!

Shaun What door?

Shaun and Bill stand in total confusion.

Dan Hi, we've not met. I'm Dan.

Julie I'm Julie. Bill was just saying he wanted us to meet.

Dan And this is Shaun.

Julie Hello, Shaun.

Shaun looks at her carefully.

Shaun Haven't we met before?

Pause.

Julie No, I don't think so.

Dan How could you have met before? Met before! Ha ha ha.

Julie So what present have you two got Bill?

Shaun still stands utterly bewildered. Dan walks forward and gives Bill the VCR.

Dan Happy viewing, Bill. Just in case you wanted to see the whole picture, so to speak.

Bill takes the VCR in his hands. He is very affected.

Bill Dan, I don't know what to say.

Dan Don't say anything.

Shaun I don't know what to say either.

Dan Then you too should maintain a discreet silence.

Bill Look, Julie. Look what my brother gave me.

Julie That's very special, Bill.

Bill Is it really mine? It's not a lend?

Dan No, it's all yours.

Bill Can I play it? Julie, you don't mind?

Dan It's second-hand, Bill. Hope that's OK. You can get such good deals second-hand these days.

Bill I like it like that. I'm a second-hand kind of guy. (*He begins to set up the video.*)

Shaun I give up.

Dan Sorry, Shaun?

Shaun I've just spent five minutes or so trying to find any explanation for what has just happened but I can't. And I'm sure we've met before.

Shaun goes towards the bathroom. Dan leaps in.

Dan Where are you going?

Shaun I need a piss.

Dan You sure?

Shaun What?

Dan Are you sure you need one? Think about it. What's telling you you need a piss?

Shaun I don't know, I just need a piss.

Dan Prove it.

Shaun What do you mean, prove it? Prove I need a piss?

Dan I'm just saying, how do you know you need to piss?

Shaun How does someone ever know they need a piss? They just need to, end of story. I don't get it, what's wrong with me having a piss?

Dan I just don't think you need one. You don't look like you need one. Does he?

Shaun Don't I?

Dan So, why are you going if you don't need one? Are you feeling like pissing now?

Shaun I don't know. I did!

Dan History's history, Shaun, and we are right here, right now. I am asking you a very simple question. Do you need to piss? Yes or no?

Shaun I guess not.

Pause.

Bill I'm glad that's settled. Because I do need a piss.

Dan What?

Bill All that talk of pissing made me want to go.

Dan No. Bill, Bill! I think Shaun wants to go after all.

Shaun What?

Dan Shaun, you want to go, don't you?

Shaun You just told me I didn't want to go!

Dan Well, now I think you do.

Shaun Well, I don't. One hundred per cent not. Nothing is further from my mind!

Bill I'll just be a second.

Dan Bill, wait!

Bill turns at the door.

Bill What?

Dan Just mind the gear.

Bill Right. (*He goes into the bathroom.*)

Shaun Mind the what?

Bill comes out.

Bill There is a lot of musical equipment in the bathroom.

Dan Yeah, that's ours.

Shaun There's what? (*He goes over and into the bathroom as the conversation continues.*)

Bill It was not there one hour ago.

Dan Of course it was. I put it there this morning when you were playing football.

Bill I was in that bathroom one hour ago and there was no amplifier in the bath.

Dan You must have missed it.

Bill And no guitar on the loo. And no cymbals and drum in the basin.

Dan No, Bill, it was all there.

Bill No, Dan, it was not.

Dan But, Bill, how else could they have got there?

Bill I am asking myself the same question.

Shaun comes out clutching the bass guitar. He is in love.

Dan That's your bass guitar, isn't it, Shaun?

Shaun Oh, yeah. (*He sits on the floor and begins to play quietly, unamplified.*)

Dan There you are. You must have been concentrating on something else and missed them. Maybe you were thinking about the match.

Bill Julie, when you went into the bathroom just now to fetch . . . to fetch what you fetched, did you notice anything odd about the bathroom?

Julie What do you mean, odd?

Bill Well, did you notice that there was an entire rock band's gear in the bathroom?

Pause. Dan looks at her desperately.

Julie Yes, of course.

Dan There you are.

Bill And that didn't strike you as being worthy of comment?

Julie Bill, if you recall, at the time I had my mind on other things. I made a mental note to ask you later. Then, when you mentioned to me that Dan was here and that he was the manager of a rock band, it cleared up the confusion.

Bill Dan, I think I might be unwell. I have no recollection of these instruments whereas I do have a recollection of closing the door. But the instruments are there, and the door was open.

Dan It's just memory loss, Bill. I've read about this kind of thing.

Bill Read about it?

Dan It's nothing.

Bill I'm suddenly feeling a bit odd.

Julie You're not the only one.

Bill It's all this going out. I'm doing too much too quickly.

Dan Sit down, Bill. Relax.

Bill I think I need a doctor.

Dan No, you don't, Bill. You just need a nice sit down in front of your new video.

Bill Do I?

Dan Trust me. Julie, put on the video.

Bill Yes, I need something solid in my life.

Julie pauses by the video. She looks at Shaun, who is strumming.

Julie Excuse me.

Shaun (*looking up*) Yes?

Julie Where did you get this video recorder?

Shaun (*pause*) From a video recorder shop. From a shop that sells video recorders.

Julie This is my video recorder.

Pause.

Shaun No, it's not.

Julie No, it is, it's got my name on it. On the side, where I stuck the label. Look.

Bill Dan, please, what is going on?

Shaun comes over and looks.

Shaun What's your name?

Julie Julie Evans.

Shaun That's the name on here.

Julie I know.

Shaun Dan? Dan?!!

Dan Julie Evans is a common name. It could be another Julie Evans.

Julie But I doubt if there are many Julie Evans who live at the address written here.

Shaun (*reads*) 35 Vicarage Road.

Julie This video was in my living room in 35 Vicarage Road earlier today.

Beat.

Dan Shaun, I hate you. I fucking hate you, Shaun.

Shaun It's not my fault! It was you told me to get it. 'Here, Shaun, have absolutely no money, now go and get me a video recorder.' What was I supposed to do?!

Dan What is it about you, Shaun, that you get everything wrong?!

Shaun They were out! I was ingenious, I went near the football ground, thought they'd be at the game. The window was open. I was being entrepreneurial! I could have been arrested! How was I supposed to know the owner of the house would be by a one-in-a-million chance playing weird games with your brother? It was just really bad luck!

Dan You are bad luck! You are six foot of pure fucking

misfortune! Ever since you joined this band, we've been cursed! I should have got rid of you years ago. You can't play, you can't drive, you can't do anything! (*He looks around.*) I can explain. I can explain.

Julie Explain away.

Dan I wanted to get Bill a VCR.

Bill Can't you afford to buy a second-hand video?

Dan Not a whole one.

Bill What about all the money from the band?

Dan It's all locked up. In assets.

Shaun It's all locked up in Tranmere.

Dan Shut up.

Julie What's locked up in Tranmere?

Dan Nothing.

Shaun No, nothing. Only our instruments, our future, our life.

Dan You're fired.

Julie Dan.

Dan You are fired. You are no longer the bassist of Goldilox.

Bill Aren't those your instruments?

Dan . . .

Bill Whose are they?

  Pause.

Dan . . .

Julie They're Cusp's.

68

Bill They're whose?

Shaun Oh my Christ. (*He wanders into the bathroom.*)

Julie What have you done?

Bill Dan, you've got to help me out here.

Dan It's not a problem. We just kind of lost our instruments in Tranmere.

Bill Lost them?

Dan Yes, it happens. You remember I used to work at the Colosseum. Used to look after the support bands. Well, I've still got all the keys to the building. I thought I could borrow some gear. Just for a little while, just to get us back on our feet. So Tim and I drove down there. And when we'd got there, Cusp's instruments were just inside. And Cusp are so crap, Bill, they are just so the worst, most fraudulent bunch of cheating wankers in the universe. So we nicked their instruments.

Bill Cusp's instruments are in my bathroom.

Shaun comes out.

Shaun Travis Dickson's guitar is on the loo.

Julie Who's Tim?

Pause.

Shaun Where is he?

Dan He's fine. I just lost touch with him.

Shaun You what? He's blind!

Dan On our way out he was carrying the bass drum, I got too far ahead and when I turned around he was gone. He'll be fine!

Shaun He's been caught!

Dan He'll get here.

Shaun He's been arrested!

Dan He'll be fine.

Shaun He'll be banged up!

Dan What could I do?! WE HAVE NOTHING. WE ARE
NOTHING. I HAD TO DO SOMETHING! WHAT
HAVE YOU DONE? WHAT HAVE YOU DONE?
WHAT HAVE YOU EVER DONE?!!

Beat.

Bill Dan. Isn't Goldilox a big success?

Dan It's doing OK.

Bill What about your letters?

Dan I may have misrepresented the situation slightly.

Bill Did you play to over a thousand in Manchester in
January?

Shaun What?

Bill Did you play to over a thousand in Manchester?

Dan Not exactly, no.

Bill Weren't you offered a tour of Chile which you
refused for political reasons?

Shaun Oh my Christ.

Dan . . .

Bill What else?

Dan That's it. I just embellished.

Bill Is Josette meeting you for the gig in Bristol?

Dan . . .

Bill Is Josette still in the band?

Dan . . .

Bill Do you have a gig in Bristol?

Dan Yes! Yes, we do. That's the whole point! If we could just get to Bristol!

Bill Haven't you got any money at all?

Dan . . .

Bill Dan? Did you come here to see me? Me, Bill?

Dan Of course I did.

Bill Did you come here to see me, or did you come here because I was somewhere to stay? Somewhere free, the last place on earth that would take you in.

Dan No!

Bill The last place on this fucking earth that you had left to go to. The last resort. Is that all I am?

Dan Bill, everything was going so well.

Bill Did you come here to see me for myself or not. Was I the reason you came? Answer me!

Pause.

Dan No. (*Pause.*) Bill.

Bill Don't talk to me.

Dan Bill!

Bill You lied to me, played your pipe. And I got up, and I talked and danced to your tune, and began to live again. And all for nothing. For lies!

Dan I was doing it for you, Bill. I just wanted to do something for you.

71

They all stand or sit silently.

What am I going to do?

Julie Go and give everything back. Explain that you got carried away, that you went a little crazy and now you're OK.

Dan Say that to them? Never.

Julie You have to.

Dan I have my pride.

Julie You have no choice.

Dan Why does Travis Dickson have a choice? Why does Travis Dickson have a choice and I do not have a choice? Who decided he had a choice and I don't? (*to God*) Oy! Can't you see that Travis Dickson is a fraud? What are you, tone deaf?!

Bill Dan, don't.

Dan Why not?!

Bill Leave it.

Dan I don't want to leave it. I'm sick of leaving it! I'm being shafted and I want to know why!!

Bill Don't open that box. There's no bottom.

Pause.

Dan There was one time, Bill. We really nearly made it. I swear.

Bill Yeah.

Dan We were doing a gig in Birmingham, about two years ago, Barry, Barry used to play bass before Shaun, Barry knew a guy there who loved us, and he was bringing all these people from London. Big people who wanted to sign us. On the day there was a storm. The club we were playing at was underground. It got flooded under two feet of water. Cancelled. Name of the club? Noah's. Yeah. Three days later Barry left.

A groan of despair from the football crowd, and a silence.

Bill Goal.

Julie For us?

Bill For them. One–nil to them.

Shaun suddenly bursts into tears. He weeps and clutches his bass guitar.

Dan Shaun, don't cry. Please don't cry, you don't do it very well.

Shaun It's all my fault.

Dan What?

Shaun What you just said, how you nearly made it with Barry, it's true. And then I came and it's been downhill ever since. And now Josette's gone solo, Tim's in the clanger and it's all my fault. It's me. I am cursed. I AM CURSED.

Dan Shaun, you may not be blessed with all that much, but you're not cursed.

Shaun It's what my mother always said. I've never been anything but a walking disaster area and it's not fair that you should suffer any more. You were doing fine until I arrived. My mother was doing fine until I arrived. The world was a better place without me, Dan.

Dan How do you know that?

Shaun I do know. All I ever hear from people is how

73

everything used to be better in the old days. Well, that's not true for me. It's always been shit. So it must be that I brought all the shit with me and if I went away everything would be all right again. I'll go now and you'll see. Things will suddenly look brighter.

Dan What, where will you go? Shaun! Wait!

Bill Renaissance Man!

Shaun Don't call me that! I know you only call me that because I'm useless at absolutely everything. It's true. I was born with only one talent – to fuck up everybody's life who I meet. Look at today! All I do is ruin everything. Well, not any more! Let me go. Let me go!

   Dan is barring the way.

Dan No, Shaun, you mustn't. You might do something silly!

Shaun Like what?

Dan I don't know. You might harm yourself.

Shaun I hope so, I am going to jump off a bridge.

Dan What?!

Shaun You'll see, Dan, when I'm gone, there will be this rainbow, and the sun will filter through into your life like a cascade of diamonds. I want to, Dan, I want to throw myself off a bridge!

Dan I won't let you!

Shaun I want you to live in a post-Shaun world! I want you to know what that's like!

Dan I forbid you!

Shaun You can't!

Dan I do. I am your manager.

Shaun You sacked me!

Dan I reinstate you!

Shaun Impossible!

Dan You are our bassist!

Shaun I refuse!

Dan You are Goldilox's bassist!

Shaun I am nobody's bassist! I am despair, I am death. I must be destroyed!

Dan Shaun, don't! Don't!

Julie What's that noise?

Above the crowd there is a distant rhythmic banging.

Dan It's him. It's him!

Shaun Who?

Dan It's Tim! He's banging his drum. He's calling us!

They run out. The banging continues in the distance.

Julie Always drama on the last day of the season.

Bill Julie.

Julie Yeah.

Bill Do you think failure's genetic?

Julie I don't know, Bill.

Bill You see, I've been under the impression my brother was something of a sensational success. That's not really the case, is it?

Julie Apparently not.

Bill So why did he lie to me?

Julie He didn't want to disappoint you.

Bill He disappointed me by lying.

Julie Bill, he was always going to disappoint you.

Bill What you talking about?

Julie He's been living for you, Bill. He's got to stop doing everything for you while you sit here watching the damp drain down the walls. You've got to start living for yourself.

Bill I am living!

Julie Oh yeah, you and moss. I'm talking about living, real life. Look at you since he's got back. He's been like insulin thrust into your veins. You're playing football, you're running to the shops, you've even become a bit of a handsome old bastard. But he'll be gone soon. What are you going to do then? Back to the armchair and playing spot-the-calf-muscle on the TV?

Pause.

Bill I'll move

Julie Good.

Bill I will. I'll move. I'm sick of this place.

Julie Of course you are!

Bill If Dan can get out of his mess, I can get out of mine!

Julie Of course you can. You can do better than this.

Bill I'm sick of living on my own!

Julie So where will you go?

Bill Julie, I think I know what you're saying.

Julie Good.

Bill You really mean it, Julie?

Julie Mean what?

Bill Can I really?

Julie Really what?

Bill Move in with you and Amy.

Julie Sorry?

Bill We can start a new life.

Julie Bill, what makes you think we're ready for that?

Bill We've been seeing each other for two years.

Julie For two hours every Saturday. By that calculation Desmond Lynam and Alan Hansen should be thinking about sharing a little place together.

Bill Marry me.

Julie What? No, we've taken a wrong turning somewhere.

Bill Marry me.

Julie Oh my God.

Bill Please say yes.

Julie Listen, I'm going. The address is on the video. Come round when you're sane.

Bill Julie, wait.

Julie Don't play games with my life!

Pause.

Bill You don't want to be with me.

Julie It's not that.

77

Bill You don't love me.

Julie It's not that I don't love you.

Bill What then?

Julie It's just there's things we don't know about each other! There's things you don't know about me!

Bill What about the things I do know?

Julie What things?

Bill I don't know, that you like Spanish wine, and you have a mole on your left breast, and size-five feet, and you grimace when you feel pleasure, and you love your daughter and wish you could speak to her more, and you're a mean darts player, and you wish you could travel more, and you hated your father, and you love your dog, and you have a thing about condensed milk, and you are convinced you have BSE, and you are the one person in the world who could make me happy.

Julie You're mad.

Bill You're beautiful.

They kiss.

So? What do you say?

The whistle goes in the background.

Julie Full time.

Bill We lost. We're down.

The banging gets suddenly louder. Through the door comes Tim. He is bruised and bloodstained, blind, sweaty, and shaking. He continues to bang for a while, then stops. Rushing in after him, Dan and Shaun. They hug and surround him.

Dan He's here!

Tim Is that you, Dan?

Dan It's me. It's me. And here's Shaun!

Shaun Hi, Tim! It's me – Shaun.

Dan You made it. You miracle! You wonderful miracle!

Tim Can I sit down?

Dan Of course you can!

Tim sits down.

So? What? How?

Tim I lost you outside the Colosseum. I was holding this bass drum. I didn't know what to do. Then I realized that you had gone and that I would have to find my own way. I walked for miles. I couldn't see anything. I ended up in this huge building. It had a marble mosaic floor and a ceiling made of glass. And there were these figures rushing around in it carrying bags. I couldn't get out, Dan. I kept going up stairs and down stairs, up lifts and down escalators. I was so lost. It all looked the same. Then I went up to this small figure who was eating an ice cream. She said maybe I should bang my drum and you would come and find me. I wanted to thank her but then a bigger figure arrived and told the small figure not to talk to strangers. I started banging and walking. It wasn't easy. These figures kept shouting at me to keep the noise down. Then three bigger figures in uniform came up. They threw me out the building, Dan. They said I was a menace to society and dumped me in a multi-storey car park. I kept going up and down the levels, going round and round all these spirals. Then, when I did find the exit sign, I got run over. On the ring road. I was bleeding, Dan, bleeding and hurting. I just walked and walked across roads, along alleyways, just banging my drum. I was just beginning to lose hope when I saw four great beacons high in the sky. At first they were distant and strange but then they became closer and closer until I could make out what they were. They were the floodlights of the football ground. I heard the roar of the crowd. It was the most wonderful sound, like a huge river breaking into the sea. I knew then that I was close and that I would get home. I knew I'd found you, Dan.

Dan pulls out his mobile phone and dials.

Dan Josette? It's Dan. Wait! I've got the instruments. Never mind how, the point is, the gig is still on. It's Bristol, Josette. It's Bristol, it's Monday, and I am literally on my knees begging you to give it one more chance. (*Pause.*) Well, no, not literally, literally on my knees. All right, Josette. (*He gets on his knees.*) I am now on my knees. Please, Josette. I am on my knees. (*Pause.*) Thank you. Thank you. Thank you. (*He hangs up.*)

Shaun She's doing it!

Dan She's doing it!

Tim, Shaun and Dan She's doing it!

Dan We're a band. We're a band again.

Shaun We are Goldilox.

Dan Let's get going. (*He sees Bill, slows.*) Bill, we may have to leave sooner than expected. It's perhaps not wise for us to stick around too long.

Bill Go, Dan. Go for it. Don't worry about me.

Dan Bill, I was thinking. Maybe it's good you know the truth. Maybe we'll do better now. I feel free for the first time in my life.

Bill So do I, Dan.

Dan You do?

Bill Before you go. There's something I want you to hear.

Julie Bill, what are you doing?

Bill You see, Julie and I, we've been seeing each other for quite a while.

Julie No, Bill, not now. Please trust me, this is not the right time.

Bill gets on his knees.

What are you doing?

Bill Julie, will you marry me?

Dan Oh my God.

Bill Julie?

Tim has approached Julie.

Tim (*to Julie*) I know you.

Shaun That's what I said.

Dan No, I don't think so.

Tim I do, I know you.

Dan Tim, shut it will you?

Pause. Tim is up close to overcome his poor eyes.

Julie (*to Tim*) Will you go away!

Bill Julie. Please, say yes!

Julie (*to Bill*) What is wrong with you? (*to Tim*) Will you get off! (*to Bill*) It's not that simple!!

Bill Why not?!!

Tim You're the woman that slept with Dan in Tenby.

   Pause.

Shaun It is. It's her. I knew it!

   Pause.

Bill Is that true?

Julie (Yes).

Bill Dan?

Dan It was two years ago. Before you met. One night.

Bill Why didn't you tell me?

Dan I didn't know how to.

Bill What's going on?

Dan Nothing! Bill, she loves you!

Bill Does she?

Dan Tell him.

Julie Tell him what?

Dan Tell him you love him.

Julie I don't know if I love anyone.

Dan No, Bill.

Bill Shut up! You ruin everything! You take everything that's mine and you ruin it!

Dan What are you talking about? I haven't even been here!

Bill Too right. I was fine before you came back!

Dan Oh, sure you were. Aside from never leaving the house you were just dandy.

Bill And did it occur to you you might have something to do with that? Three letters in six years! What kind of brother is that?

Dan I'm sorry. I just had to get away.

Bill Away from what?

Dan Look around you! From this! From you!!

Bill From me? What did I do?

Dan Forget it.

Bill No, I want to know.

Dan All right. You made my life impossible. I couldn't do anything that would make me better than you. I had to do nothing! I had to be nothing!

Bill And what, now you're something, are you? Goldilox – the great fucking fairy tale! Look at you. Big bear, middle bear and little bear. And Goldilocks herself. Where the fuck is she? That's what I stopped you achieving, is it?

Julie It's not his fault, Bill.

Bill I just wanted something to myself. Is that too much to ask? But he won't let me have anything! Even you!

Dan It was two years ago!

Bill She's mine!

Dan It was two years! Today was just . . . (*He stops himself, but too late. Pause.*)

Bill Jesus Christ. He came back to see you, not me.

Julie Oh, for God's sake.

Bill You never loved me. You loved him. You were using me.

83

Julie Leave it out.

Dan Bill, it's pure chance.

Bill You were waiting for him. It was all planned.

Julie Don't be so stupid!

Bill Off to Bristol are you?

Julie Fuck you.

Bill Groupie. You know he's shagging Goldilocks, don't you?

Julie Forget it.

Bill Don't like being two-timed, do you?

Julie You shit.

Bill I offered you myself. And you didn't even care! You never cared!

Julie What did you say?

Dan Listen, let's calm down.

Julie I've been coming to this shithole for two years! Does that sound like not caring?! Did you ever think of that?! Did it ever cross your thick, self-centred mind that to come to this godforsaken pit every week for two years I must care for the sad bastard living in it?!

Dan Listen.

Bill You lied to me!

Julie No, you lied!

Bill I lied!

Julie You told him I was twenty-two! You told him I was platinum! You made me sound like a teenage bimbo!

Dan Listen to me! I can't stand it. I just can't stand it! It was two years ago! I was pissed! She was pissed! We just about managed to do it against a sea wall in the pissing rain. She puked on me. I was so pissed I didn't even notice. We burst into tears. She left. I passed out and woke up with my head in the sea. It's not exactly *Brief Encounter*, is it?

Bill You know what our mother told us. She said, 'The meek shall inherit the earth.' But we never do. We don't get fuck all.

Enter Amy in war-paint, looking sad. All look round.

Amy We lost . . . We're down.

Julie Really?

Amy Cusp have cancelled. They announced it after the game. They've had their instruments nicked.

Dan, Julie, Shaun and Tim Really?

Amy Just thought I'd tell you the score.

Julie Amy! I'm sorry.

Amy Yeah, one–nil. Gifted them the goal.

Julie I'm sorry about today.

Amy Nothing new. (*Pause.*) That's Cusp's bass guitar.

Pause.

Dan We should be going.

Amy You stole their instruments. I was going to that gig tonight!

Dan Yeah, sorry. We'll make it up to you. Come and see us any time. I'll put you on the guest list.

Amy I can't wait.

Dan Yeah. Come on, lads.

Tim Dan. I've got an idea.

The band go into the bathroom. Bill goes and turns the video on.

Julie Well, I'm going to go back home. Are you coming?

Amy I want to talk to Bill.

Julie What time will you be back?

Amy Don't know.

Julie Well, don't be long.

Amy I'm sixteen. I can do what I like.

Pause. Julie makes to leave. Dan comes out of the bathroom door with a plug.

Dan You're going?

Julie I think it's best. Good luck.

Dan Thanks. Bill will let you know how we're doing.

Julie . . .

Dan Well.

They shake hands.

Wait for a second. (*He returns into the bathroom.*)

Amy What's going on?

Bill Go away. Both of you. Just go away.

A sound of guitars. The band enter.

Band
Happy Birthday to you,
Happy Birthday to you,
Happy Birthday, dear Amy,

Happy Birthday to you.

Amy Thanks.

Dan No problem! Just wanted to make up for ruining your night out. (*sensing a frostiness*) Right, let's get this stuff out.

The band lead the gear out of the room.

Julie Bill, come round. Come round if you want.

Nothing from Bill. He just watches. Shaun crosses the stage with an amp, singing.

Shaun
Don't tell me
I'm not free
Ba ba bee
Da da dee.

He exits.

Julie It was nothing. One night of madness. You need them and then they mean nothing . . . (*Nothing.*) Bill. Keep the video. You're going to need it.

She leaves. Amy and Bill alone on stage.

Amy Bill. I want to give you something. A present.

Bill Amy, it's your birthday, you're the one who gets the presents. I don't want it, whatever it is. Please don't give it to me. Don't give me anything!

The band return.

Dan The sun's out. Spring evening all of a sudden. Just when winter looked like it would never end. Well, here we are. I'm no expert at this sort of thing.

Shaun Goodbye is the hardest thing to say.

Amy Where are you going?

Dan Bristol. We've got our next gig in Bristol. It's been . . . it's been good.

Dan approaches Bill. Bill tenses.

Goodbye then. Are you going to wish me luck?

Bill (*emotionless*) Good luck.

Dan Thanks! Well, as I say, better make tracks. Say goodbye, Tim.

Tim Bye, Amy.

Amy I'm here, Tim.

Tim Bye. I'll miss you.

He gropes his way over and hugs her tight. Then wanders back.
Shaun follows and clumsily embraces her.

Shaun Nice one. Don't hang up the boots.

Amy I'll listen out for you on the radio.

Shaun You do that. Goldilox. With an X. Remember the name.

Amy I'll try.

Dan Right, have we got everything? Feel like we've been here for a month and it's not even a day. We'll see ourselves out. Thanks for putting us up. I think we know the way. It's a four-hour drive, should be there before dark. Straight down the M4. I've never been to Bristol. No idea where we'll stay but that's what it's all about, on the road. It's got warmer, has it? Spring is in the air. Watford in the spring, I remember it's quite different. Everyone blossoms like flowers. Late this year. We seem to be finding it hard to actually leave.

Bill Try the door.

Dan Yes, come on, lads, out we go.

The band slowly meander out of the door, Shaun lead-
ing Tim. Dan stops in the door.

Bill?

Bill Say it, Dan.

Dan Nothing. Up the Hornets.

He leaves and shuts the door.
   Bill doesn't move.
   Amy looks at him for a while, then pulls out a piece
of paper and reads out loud.

Amy April 25th, 1996. Vicarage Road, Watford. Watford
0, Leicester 1. Match report by Amy Evans.
   Watford Football Club was relegated today, losing a
game they had to win to survive in the first division. In an
afternoon that captured in its ninety minutes the sad
decline of a once great club, eleven men in gold were
gradually ground down by a Leicester side that were
stronger, fitter and more experienced. At times one could
see the ghosts of great Watford players of the past wandering the pitch in a helpless lament for former glories: a
half-shadow of John Barnes floating up and down the left
wing, or the spirit of Ross Jenkins perched like a gloomy
tower on his favourite six-yard line waiting for a cross
that never came. All over the pitch spirits and ghosts
could be seen as if rising one last time to pay tribute to
their once beloved club.
   The goal came from a Leicester header. As Hornets
goalkeeper Kevin Miller dived in vain to push the ball
away, one could make out in shadow behind him the
giant frame of Steve Sherwood stretching his six foot five
inches to try to guide the ball wide. You could feel the

agony as the ball passed through Sherwood's ghostly flesh and hit the back of the net for the only goal of the game. Almost immediately Watford supporters and spirits began slowly to file away like mourners from a funeral. The final minutes were played out to a sad silence. Watford are down. Long live Watford.

This is this reporter's one-hundred-and-thirty-first report on Watford Football Club. It is also my last. It has been an honour to serve this club but I will not be writing any more.

Amy Evans.

Amy goes over and tries to give Bill the piece of paper.

Bill Last game?

Amy Everything has to end some time. Take it.

Bill What about your father? Send it to him.

Amy He's got enough.

Bill He should have the complete collection.

Amy I don't even know if he's alive. He's never written back. I've sent him a report once a week for five years and I've heard nothing. I want you to have it.

Bill Maybe he's moved?

Amy I don't care.

Bill He's your father.

Amy So what? I've waited five years for him, hoping he would come back. But he's not going to. Take it.

Bill takes it.

Look after it. It's my final work.

Bill Thank you.

Amy I'm off.

Bill Good.

Amy Maybe we can have another kickaround some time.

Bill Got to get over this injury.

Amy OK. Find me when you're ready.

Bill I will. I will.

Amy Have you noticed how when people say something twice, it means it's not true.

Bill No, I will . . . I will.

Amy goes to the door. She pauses, not wanting to go. Bill is looking at the paper. Amy opens the door.

Amy? Next season. I was thinking. You still thinking of going?

Amy Why?

Bill Nothing. Just thought if you were . . .

Amy Yeah?

Bill Well, I might tag along.

Amy You mean it?

Bill Nothing like a new season.

Amy Elton John and Graham Taylor are back.

Bill Who knows? Might get promotion.

Amy August 18th. I'll pick you up.

Bill Two-thirty?

Amy Two-thirty. I'll bring you a scarf.

Bill No. I've got my own.

He holds it up.
Amy opens the door.

Amy It's sunny.

Bill How did that happen?

She goes out and closes the door behind her.
A silence as Bill once again finds himself alone.
Bill holds the piece of paper in his hand. He reads it slowly. He is filled with a new, good emotion. The roar of a cheering crowd returns in his mind. It is a mighty sound.